Grandmothers are Forever

*Poems, Words, and Thoughts for, and from,
a Grandmothers Undying Love*

Rebecca Grace Cunningham
Rachael Faith Cunningham
Sarah James Cunningham

Copyright © 2016 by Randall Sorbel

All rights reserved. No part of this publication may be reproduced, distributed, or transmitted in any form or by any means, including photocopying, recording, or other electronic or mechanical methods, without the prior written permission of the publisher, except in the case of brief quotations embodied in critical reviews and certain other noncommercial uses permitted by copyright law. For permission requests, write to the publisher, addressed "Attention: Permissions Coordinator," at the address below.

Randall Sorbel
18571 Buena Vista Ave
Yorba Linda, CA 92886

Printed in the United States of America

Publisher's Cataloging-in-Publication data
Sorbel, Randall
Grandmothers are Forever : Poems, Letters, and Ruminations, For, and From, A Grandmother's Undying Love / Randall Sorbel ; with Rebbeca Cunningham, Rachael Cunningham, and Sarah Cunningham
p. cm.
ISBN 978-0692801093

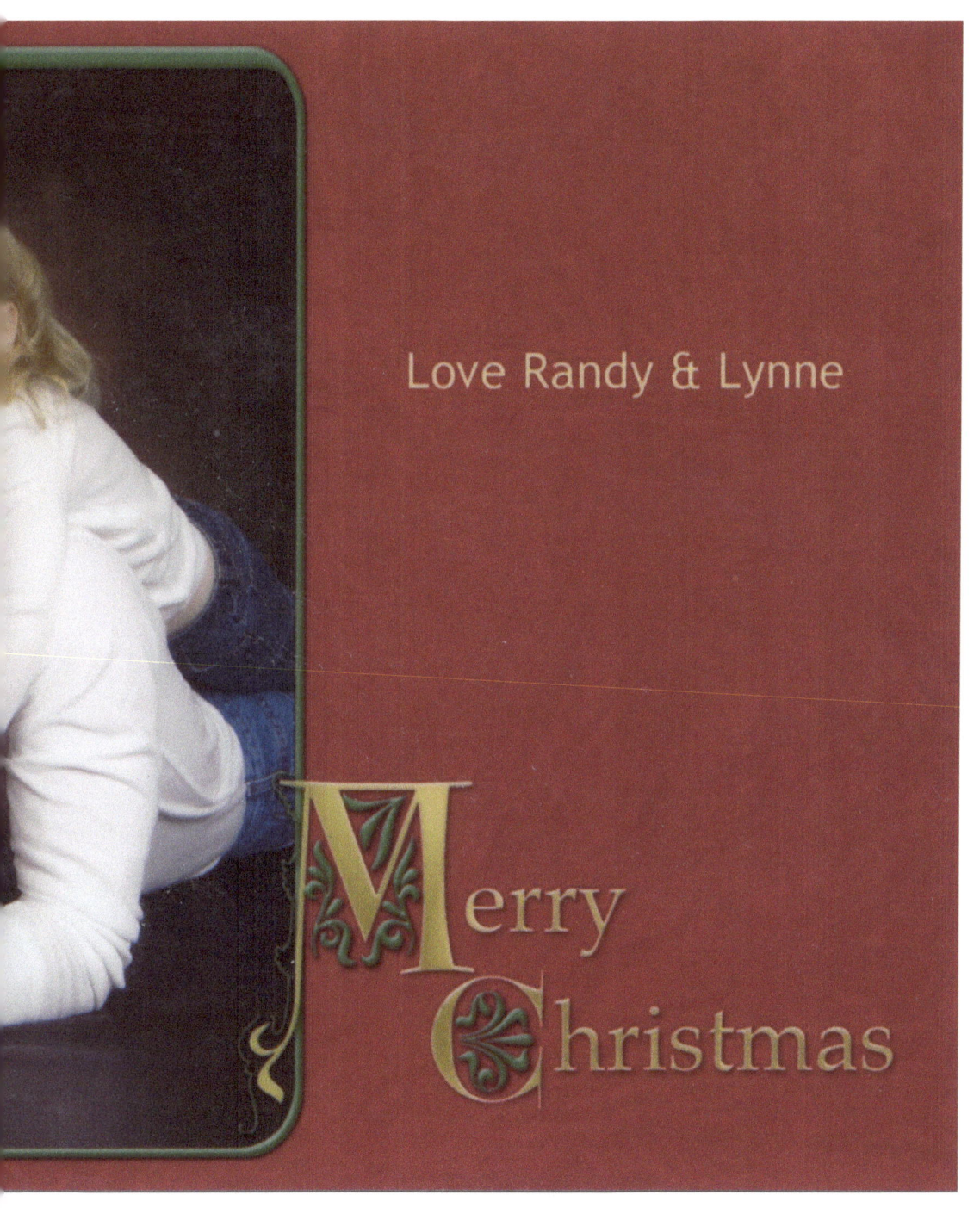

Love Randy & Lynne

Merry Christmas

To My Grandchildren

We can buy treasures at most any store.
We can order online precious items galore.
But we'll only find true treasure in the blue of your eyes.
It's holding you and loving you.
There, our real treasure lies.

Our hearts can be fickle.
We love many things.
The world shows us treasure we think that we need.
The day you were born our hearts felt true love.
It's a gift from our God and it comes from above.

Precious jewels and boxed candy
In heart shapes are nice.
These worldly treasures can deceive us.
It's best to look twice.
Every year you grow older our hearts need to grow.
For our love grows right with you. We pray that you know.

Lynne Sorbel
<u>To My Grandchildren</u>

Introduction

I feel honored that my granddaughters have asked me to write this introduction to their book on their Grandma Lulu. This book is a testimony of their and other peoples' love for her. This is a story that anyone can love, for there is no better way to celebrate Lynne Sorbel's life than a wonderful tribute to her through the eyes of her grandchildren. I believe this book immortalizes the grandmother's role – loving, understanding, non-judgmental, and a perfect listener. She was their rock and always had time to be anywhere for them. She left us too soon, at 56 years on Christmas Eve, 2014.

Lynne and I were married for over twenty years and even though she wasn't a biological grandparent, she fit and cherished this role perfectly with her loving grandchildren.

Born on June 13, 1958, Lynne started suffering pain and sickness a few years before her death. Despite this, she was vibrant, determined, loving, and a beautiful lady. And even though she was stunning, her true beauty came from within. A strong Christian, she always wanted to help people in need. Yes, her life was an open book for all to read and a light went out in our lives when she left us. It is just as hard being without her today as it was the first day. I'm so sorry that I couldn't ease her pain, and I thought my love would keep her with us. Lynne battled massive migraines for several years, but the last two were especially difficult for her. We all miss her kisses and hugs more than anything, and the three granddaughters (Rebecca, Rachael, and Sarah) who authored this book, couldn't wait to ask for private time to discuss the preteen and teen issues of the day, what they referred to as "important girl talk." Her smile and demeanor would light up the room, and even if she didn't know you, she would make you feel comfortable. She will always be the guardian angel to her grandchildren, Rebecca, Rachael, Sarah, Mia, and Skylar. I know I speak for all who loved her – "I would give anything to be with her just one more day." Rest assured my love; we will see you again – all in God's time – and oh, what a joyous time that will be!

It has been said, and it is so true – "You don't know about lonely until it's chiseled in stone."

Randall Sorbel
Husband of Lynne Sorbel

To My Husband

Dearest Randy,

I am so sorry I am not with you today as you celebrate Father's Day – because to me, you represent "fathers" in all the best ways that I can think of. You give of yourself for others – always – not just when you 'feel" like it. You are loving and kind even when we don't deserve it!

Thank you for who you are and all you do to represent our Heavenly Father here on earth. I love you with all my heart.

Always and forever,
Your "Love",

Lynne

To my Husband

To my heart's content, my mind's eye, my life's love...

to the times we've had, the times we're having, the times yet to come...

2011

Thank you for who you are and all you do to represent our Heavenly Father here on earth! I love you with all my heart.

always & forever,
your "love", Lynne ♡

Dearest Randy,   6-17-11

I am so sorry I

Thank you for being such a great husband.

Happy Father's Day, with all my love.

am not with you today as you celebrate Father's Day because to me you represent "fathers" in all the best ways I can think of. You give of yourself for others – always – not just when you "feel" like it. You are loving and kind even when we don't deserve it!

Lynne – A Life Story

Lynne Marie Sorbel, often affectionately referred to as Lulu, was born on June 13, 1958, to Edward and Jeanne Dunne. Lynne's father was a Cardiologist; her mother is a former schoolteacher. Her father passed away several years ago, but her mother is still with us.

Lynne certainly took after her parents as she always touched the hearts of those in her life and taught us all so many valuable things by the way she lived her life. Lynne has seven siblings – Edward, Leslie, Carrie, Janice, Mer, Denice, and Kathy.

As Lynne started school, it became obvious that she was an outstanding student, continually getting straight A's. This pattern of academic achievement continued through college and graduate school at UCLA. After the completion of her master degree, Lynne became a therapist for abused children and a counselor for adults.

Lynne was truly caring and compassionate. To know her was to love her, and when Lynne knew you – you felt deeply loved. When Randy first met Lynne, he knew she was different and yet at the same time, so humble. She made everyone feel special and of course, we all wanted to be around her.

She loved traveling with Randy around the country and to their vacation home in Brookings, Oregon, but could never get home fast enough to see her beloved grandchildren. They all were truly cherished by her, and she never failed to mention and constantly express her love for them. Lynne became a Born-Again Christian over 20 years ago, and was devoted to her Lord and Savior Jesus Christ, and now she has gone home to enjoy His presence for all eternity. Her daily Bible reading brought her great happiness and enlightenment. She continued reading towards the end of her life; even though she had trouble seeing and suffered from severe migraine headaches. Whenever she was out and about, she would always share her love for Jesus by showing compassion and extreme generosity towards those whom she loved and strangers alike. Lynne loved to share with others her salvation and redemption by God's grace.

Lynne and Randy were married for over 20 years and enjoyed a beautiful, loving relationship. It's Randy's hope that everyone here would experience what they shared together. He misses her dearly and loves her so much. It brings Randy great peace knowing Lynne is now with Jesus rejoicing and pain-free.

The White Sheep

Coming from a family of eight, it was often easy to get lost in the shuffle. Growing up, while there was lots of love flowing around, it was difficult for any ONE of us to feel that we were special all the time. However, now that we are all adults, many of us with children of our own, I think we all realize that Mom and Dad were doing the bet they could given the large number of us – quite literally, they were outnumbered in any case. It is amazing that not only did we all survive, but also we managed to foster our unique personalities and have a great love for one another.

The oldest of eight, I never dreamt, in a million years, that I would be sitting here today writing about my little sister who passed away at the young age of 56. I just always assume that I would be the first to go. The sadness and grief are overwhelming at times – all the "what-ifs" constantly running through my mind.

Lynne, (Lulu, Lulubelle, Lynnie) was the third in line. After me, there was our brother Ed, then Lynne, then four more sisters, (Kat, Carrie, Neese, Beebs), and finally, a baby brother, Ryan. The four oldest naturally fell into what we called the "Big Guys", and the four youngest were the "Little Guys." At the time that Lynne was born, Mom and Dad had moved with Ed and me from Washington D.C., to a small house they rented in Eagle Rock, California. Ed and I each had full sized cribs, which were put in a large walk in closet. Lynne slept in a small portable crib in the bathroom next to Mom and Dad's room. They were obviously right quarters, so Mom and Dad had a house built for our growing brood in the Los Feliz area of Los Angeles. It was a four-bedroom house with a den that became Ed's bedroom, and eventually an add-on attic bedroom. This is the home where we all grew up. Many of our fondest memories revolve around our time in that home, and as adults, we drive by the old house, (which is still pretty much) to show our kids and to reminisce fondly.

In the early years, Lynne and I were the best of buds. We played make believe together; loved our Thumbelina dolls, enjoyed the swings in the back yard, read Nancy Drew books with our neighbor friend, swam at Jude's house almost every day in the summer and played dress-up with Mom's clothes, and so on. Eventually, we took guitar lessons and sewing lessons. Lynne always seemed to shine in whatever she did. Besides always being the straight-A student, I just thought she was naturally more gifted than I was at everything. However, I now realize a lot of it was that she was always approached anything new with incredible enthusiasm and determination to succeed. And yet, she was not competitive with others. I remember once, in sewing class, I made my first dress with a zipper. After struggling with it for hours it seemed, I was so proud to have finally it completed. When I held it up to admire, I saw to my horror that the zipper was completely crooked. Lynne immediately offered to help me fix it, which she did with no trouble!

Lynne was also never one to procrastinate. Whereas I, and most probably most of the rest of the population of the world, put off doing something that presents any challenge. Lynne, on the other hand, always dove right in immediately and did what needed to be done. If she had the assignment to do a report due in 3 weeks, she insisted that Mom take her to the library that same day, so she could get all the books she needed to get started! Then she would begin her research immediately and complete that report within days while the rest of her class, no doubt, hadn't even decided on their report topic yet. In high school, I remember some of her friends begging her to help them with their reports or papers since she was already done with hers – and she always did, the generous spirit that she was. And, I'm pretty sure, they all got A's! Lynne didn't have a competitive bone in her body, always happy for others' successes and quick to give praise.

As more kids came along, (just about one every year!) Lynne and I, as the two elder sisters, were expected to help with the younger kids. We helped give them baths, change diapers, and feed with bottles. As the kids all grew, we would obviously play with them as well – some of our fondest memories revolved around putting on "plays" for our parents on Sunday evenings. All the girls would put on one of Mom's fancy negligees (with many safety pins to hold them up!) and Lynne, and I would carefully apply Mom's makeup for everyone. We would take turns holding up a sheet across the living room entrance for scene changes. I'm not sure there was much talent involved, but we sure had a lot of fun, and imagined that our audience was thoroughly entertained!

Our sister, Lynne, was always a very generous soul. Kat remembers her big sister patiently teaching her to "pick" on the guitar and master special strums that she knew, as well as endlessly driving Kat and her friends across town. Of course, when Lynne let Kat have the coveted attic bedroom a few years early while she went back to sharing a room with one of the Little Guys.

Of course, every sibling is full of memories that illustrated the beauty of Lynne, from her generosity to her selflessness. Even our children loved their Aunt Lulu. It was simply her nature, to love and be loved. You will live on in our hearts and minds forever.

Overall, our dear sister Lynne was a very sweet, loving, and generous, and spiritual person. Ironically, growing up I remember thinking that sometimes she was sort of the "black sheep" of the family – she was not as overtly funny, loud, silly, or competitive, vying for the attention of those around her. She was a quiet, sensitive, gentle soul. I realize now that maybe we were all the black sheep, and she was the one "White Sheep". Truer words could not be said of Lynne – she was the most selfless person that I knew, a spirit whose loving ways will never be forgotten.

We all love you, Lulu, and wish we had more time with you here on this Earth to show you much you meant to us. We think of you every day and look forward to seeing you again in Heaven someday (if any of us make it!)

Words From a Friend

I'm Carin Call-Faqua, and Lynne was my best friend. We met in 1972 at Immaculate Heart High School. From this moment on, for the next four years, we were pretty much inseparable. Lynne was blessed with a large family, and including Lynne, there was a total seven sisters and one brother. She introduced me to her entire family, and I felt as If I were the eighth sister. The Dunne home was similar to a college sorority, with lots of laughter, some sibling rivalry, but most of all, love. Lynne's siblings all had nicknames: Les for Leslie, Lulu for Lynne, Kat for Kathy, Care for Carrie, Neese for Denise, Beebs for Janice, Mer for Mary, and, of course, Eddy for Ed. Les, Lulu, and Kat were the mini-mommies of the family. With seven girls, Mrs. Dunne needed all the help she could get!

When Lynne got her driver's license, Mrs. Dunne promptly requested she act as the designated driver for the four younger sisters. She drove her Mom's bucket of bolts station wagon and loved every second of driving her younger sisters to and from wherever they needed to go. Lynne was a petite young lady, and if you could imagine how she looked in this station wagon, with the steering wheel the size of a hula-hoop, you would all have a good laugh. She always had the radio blaring and would sing along to her favorites – James Taylor, Kenny Loggins, Simon and Garfunkel, and Joni Mitchell. Lulu had a beautiful voice, like an angel, singing her heart out every chance that she could. Her favorite casual, "driving around in the station wagon attire", were Farmer-John overalls. For those of you who have only known Lynne as an adult, I'm sure you cannot even begin to picture Lynne in these frumpy overalls.

Lynne and her sisters helped their father, Dr. Dunne, with his radiology practice by transcribing his medical records. They were all trained by Leslie and Lynne, and it always fascinated me how the knowledgable they were. It's no wonder that four of them became nurses, and I always that Lynne would be a great doctor.

Lynne was tiny, but her heart was enormous, always a kind soul and didn't have a bad word to say about anybody. Lulu was my most loyal friend and was very beautiful inside and out. My mom Diane used to call her the Dresden Doll because of her beautiful, porcelain features.

One memory that I will never forget was our junior year in high school, when twenty girls came down to our Palm Desert home for one of the most exciting spring breaks, sunbathing by the pool for five days with baby oil, iodine, foil, lemons and peroxide in our hair! Those were the golden days, my Lulu.

May the road rise up to meet you.
May the wind be always at your back.
May the sun shine warm upon your face;
The rains fall soft upon your fields, and until we meet again,
May God hold you in the palm of His hand.

Whatever the distance or the length of time between our talks, our friendship never skipped a beat. I am so thankful that she is no longer in pain and suffering. Lynne, I love and will miss you forever and always.

Carin Call-Faqua
Childhood Friend

Words From Tenzing

In the memory of Lynne, when I think back on the relationship we had, all I can think about was the unconditional love that we had shared which was priceless. The very first time that I met her in 2005, we had a special connection that cannot be described in words. From the moment that we met, she always treated me like her daughter and friend.

I had a wonderful relationship with her that cannot be forgotten. Lynne bestowed her love upon me, and I remember the many things that she had done for me, including helping with my wedding in 2006. She arranged a beautiful bridal shower for me, much as a sister or a best friend would have done. That touched my heart, and I still have fond memories of that until this day. Lynne also took me to her hairstylist to have my hair styled for the special day, and also helped out in other wedding necessities that were unforgettable, just as if someone would do for their daughter. I still remember her kindness until this day, and I am truly grateful.

Whenever we met or talked over the phone, there was this indescribable connection, allowing me to feel completely comfortable around her. She would always remember the little things, and my parents would always tell me she was such a beautiful person both outside and in, and their admiration reinforced my pride to have her in my life.

I miss her every day, and the beautiful memories that we shared with her are precious. I thank Lynne for being a wonderful grandmother to Skyler and Mia, and although it is unfortunate that they could not enjoy her love for many years to come, the love that she did share with them was precious and will never be forgotten. Despite the fact that the years may pass, the family will always remind the children of her undying love.

May her beautiful soul rest in peace in Heaven, smiling, looking down upon us and protecting us. We love her very much, and she will remain alive in our hearts forever.

Tenzing Sorbel
Daughter-in-Law

A Tribute to My Dear Friend

Back in the mid-1990's, I led my first Bible Study. It was a study on what the Bible had to say about marriage without regrets. I led this study in a home, and there were approximately twenty women who attended. I share this only to paint the picture of an intimate setting and how very easily I was able to look into the eyes of each woman who attended and connect with them. To my delight, this beautiful gal came to this home and sat very strategically in a place where she could see me face to face. Her name was Lynne, and she did this every week. As I got to know her I found out that she was a new Christian, newly married, and very hungry to learn about Jesus and His plan for a healthy and thriving marriage. I can still see her face in my memories of leading that study. She was joyful and so eager to apply God's ways as a newly wedded bride. We as women shared honestly the challenges and benefits to aligning to what the Bible says about begin a godly wife – and Lynne was "all in!" She was so teachable. It was such a breath of fresh air to meet this wise, educated woman who sat on the edge of her seat and took notes, asked questions and obeyed the word of God to the best of her ability. I always offered to go to lunch with anyone in the group who would like to go after the study was over. It worked out to be just Lynne and me most of the time. I look back at all those lunches with deep gratitude for all that Lynne, and I shared together over salads and tacos. Lynne and I were fast friends. We shared a kindred heart of loving God, wanting a great marriage and hungry to know what the Bible has to say about 'all life" and purposing to apply it to our lives with God's help.

One of the richest things Lynne and I shared was a personal relationship with Jesus Christ. Both of us had been exposed to "Religion" – the rituals and traditions that seem to fetter themselves to knowing God. But God in His kindness gave the world Jesus. John 3:16, a book in the Bible found in the New Testament says, "For God so loved the world that He gave His only son, that who-so-ever would believe on Him would not perish but have everlasting life." Man made religion, but God gave us Jesus so that every person could be forgiven of their sins when they placed their faith in who Jesus was and is, and trusted that He took the punishment for their sins, so that they could be right with God and have a relationship with Him. Lynne and I both moved through religion to a personal relationship with Jesus, and neither of us has ever been the same since. Truly knowing Jesus Christ brings love, joy, peace, patience, gentleness, kindness, and self-control into the fabric of every circumstance of life. He is the ultimate game changer, and He did that for Lynne's life.

As Lynne's health became more challenged and she battled so much pain through the headaches he experienced, her resolve never faltered. She would live and love to bring God glory every day that she was given.

At Lynne's memorial service a sweet joy welled up in my heart as I heard one woman after the next share about their relationship with Lynne. Truly each one of them introduced themselves by their name and would then say, "I was Lynne's best friend." It happened over and over again! It became quite the banter; one woman would stand up and share that she was Lynne's best friend. It might have seemed like a competition, but I sat back delighting in it all. This was the greatest testimony to who Lynne was. She loved deeply, and she loved well. She valued the people in her life for who they were and loved them and cherished the relationship they shared. Randy, of course, was the love of her life, and her desire was to be the best wife, lover and friend to him that she could be.

I have been richly blessed to have shared life with Lynne and to have called her a dear friend. I miss her so much, but this I am certain of, I will see her again and shared eternal life with her. She just beat me to Heaven.

Val Selvig
Friend

Special Love

Can love be contained
In a cup or a vase?
Does it grow every day
When I see your sweet face?

I don't really know,
But of one thing I am sure
The love in my heart
Is from God and it's pure.

My three precious darlings,
I love them so much.
I love their sweet giggles,
The feel of their touch.

Every day we're apart
Is so hard, this I know.
But the love in my heart
Just continues to grow.

Grandma Lulu
<u>Special Love</u>

Roses are sweet
And their petals are soft
But their sweetness will fade,
And the petals drop off.

Our love is solid.
It will never fade.
It grows every year
Its foundation is laid.

With tender care God has blessed us,
With three special girls.
Happy Valentine's Day dear ones,
Papa and I love you so much.

Rebecca

Words from Rebecca

There are no words to describe the gap in my heart that I feel because of the loss of my Grandma, Lynne Marie Dunne-Sorbel, Grandma Lulu. She was more than a grandmother and more than a friend, and although she wasn't technically related to my family, she was more than worthy to be a part of it. Never before had I met such a beautiful, caring, generous, and godly woman. Every single one of her words was specifically and carefully chosen only to benefit and bless those around her, including my sisters and me. I know that we were and are very important to her and that she loved us with all of her heart and beyond, but still I cannot help but confess a thought that has been on my mind for some time. I am the eldest child in my family, and I had the privilege to be my grandma's first "child" as well. She used to tell me stories about how when I was born, she looked at my mom and said, "Look out, this one's mine."

Ever since my childhood, we've had such a deep connection that almost seemed like a mother-daughter relationship. I always felt that we were the closest of sisters. She would take me shopping, listen to me when I was perplexed, and take me out to eat even when her head began to hurt. Come to think of it, I never really realized how blessed I was until I sat down to write this. Sure, it pains me to reminisce and long for the olden days, but I am grateful she was there to help me through some very difficult and emotional times.

There's so much I wanted to say before that I never got a chance to say. And similarly, so much has happened after you passed that I just wish I could talk to you about my life. I always had the notion that you would be there for me forever and through everything and I guess the thought of death never seemed like a plausible and conceivable idea. Now, it's "realer" and after seven months of thinking and healing and making mistakes, I think I have an idea of how to deal with it and what to think of it. When you passed, I was in so much shock...there was nothing I could say, and I spoke more through my actions which was perhaps, not the best idea. Life is a series of difficult choices, and I often came to you in search of better options. Wading through this world without your helping hand is hard to bear, and harder still to assign to a lifetime. Sometimes I just wish you could take me out, and we could just get lunch, and I could listen to you tell me stories about your childhood, about how you met Papa or even funny baby stories. Sometimes I tend to focus too much on what has been lost, rather than what has been gained, and I fail to see the whole picture. But regardless, I could never ask for a better Grandma/Mom because to me; you always were one. I love you forever from eternity to eternity. I just pray that one day people will talk about me like they speak about you. I love you, Grandma.

Grandmothers are Forever

Rebecca in a Nutshell

Rebecca is wise, a mother to her sisters, herself, and her friends, and it is this nurturing quality that fits her role, the eldest of three sisters. Music emanates from her graceful hands, yet there is a ferocity that drives her gentle eyes – she burns with intelligence beyond her years, but perhaps, befitting her experiences. She exhibits an elevated grasp of language, illustrated in her raw poetry, etchings of her soul that inscribe themselves on paper, her eyes the only witness.

She is fiercely ambitious, yet faithfully committed to her heritage, allowing the grace of her God to permeate her thoughts. Here, she finds the solace to venture towards a life of service, and she is suited more for it, than most. It is the generosity of her spirit that dictates her motivations, and in the quiet, her presence speaks volumes.

She plays on, perhaps taking the reins helps her avoid the downpour.

When I grow up, I want to either study psychology or music. I'm fascinated by psychology - riveted by how people react to certain situations, what moves people to behave the way that they do. I am fascinated by what makes an evil mind different than those who exhibit normal patterns, the relation between the brain and behavioral patterns, and why certain inputs affect individual outputs - mental diseases - - why they are passed on. I love working with people, or kids who were abused - to talk to them, understand their atmospheric conditions that lead them to reactions - struggling with drugs or doing well in school, and how they put their problems in place in life. Reactions are a choice, and I want to understand why.

Of course, my faith teaches me patience, and it is here that I would not shy away from the role of a mother, but that, too, is a balance. To study oneself, and others require dedication, and that path has dominated my mind.

Perhaps, my rougher than average childhood led me to this path, as I often ruminate on the reasons that I was forced to undergo behaviors from unaware loved ones. Rather than steep in the unfair nature of the situation, I became obsessed with determining what the engine behind those actions was – and in my quest, I realize that helping children in similar situations is the ultimate goal.

Maybe, music helps me to understand that a symphony is but an arrangement of notes, some subtle, some obvious, that can quickly degenerate into a cacophony

It's all a matter of perspective.

When God Made Rebecca

When God made Rebecca
His purpose was clear
He made her quite special
To Him she's so dear.

Her heart without blemish
She's sweet thru and thru
Our precious Becca,
We love her, it's true.

So bless and keep her Dear Father of all,
She's ours for a short time
On your mercy we call.
Protect her and guide her
And fill her with love,
Our precious Rebecca
God's gift from above.

Grandma Lulu
<u>When God Made Rebecca</u>

Dear Rebecca,

I feel like I haven't seen you in ages. You are a busy girl and I have been sick – but we have to try to have some one on one time soon.

I am having withdrawals from you, and I have to hear all the goings-on with you and your friends so far this school year.

I love you so much and am always so proud of all you do to reach out to others to share Christ and to share with us the gifts God has given you in the talent Department. You are a special girl and it's a pleasure to watch you becoming a lady. I miss you Sweetie, and I am so sorry I haven't been around.

All my love forever and ever,

Grandma Lulu
October 2013

Grandmothers are Forever

Your Soul and Your Heart

She's a fabulous girl who's
Named Becca Grace.
Intense love fills my heart
As I gaze at her face.

Her heart is so pure;
Jesus lives there full time
And each day I thank Him
That Rebecca is mine.

Seven special years ago,
On a hot summer day,
You came down from Heaven
And I started to pray.

I pray for your safety,
Your soul and your heart.
I thank God each day
You're so sweet and so smart.

Happy birthday sweet angel,
My first baby love.
May God bless you today
As He looks down from above.

Grandma Lulu
<u>Your Soul and Your Heart</u>

Rachael

Words From Rachael

Grandmothers are Forever

I love my grandma so much for so many reasons that are hard to explain. I loved how whenever I was with her I felt that I could tell her anything I wanted, and she was there to give me the affection, advice, or support I needed. Whenever I looked at her, her eyes would sparkle, and I would get this warm, happy feeling that made me feel safe and comfortable around her. Grandma Lulu was something different in a wonderful way. When you looked at her, you could tell that she was very special. No matter whom she talked to, whether she knew them or not, or whether her relationship with them was good or bad, she would treat them with respect and kindness. I remember how she would take my sisters and me shopping or to do something special with her. We would always switch off with her, and sometimes when we went to the mall together to have some grandma/granddaughter time, and she would start to feel sick, or a migraine was coming on, I realized that she was trying to push through the pain and act like everything was alright.

Even though she wasn't always feeling well, she would always make sure our needs were taken care of before anything else. Of course, she even had yummy treats that Papa wouldn't approve of, and we kept those moments a secret.

I would and will always think of her as a second Mom, doing everything for me that she could. I will never forget her, and all the wonderful things she has done for my family and me.

Although she wasn't my Grandma by blood, I would never let that make a difference in our relationship. Related by blood or not, she was the person I loved before, and will always.

Rachael in a Nutshell

Rachael cheers. She cheers people up; she cheers on her peers, and she cheers as a sport. Of course, passion is what drives her, this commitment to the art of gymnastics. Perhaps, it is her flexible nature that moves this goal towards perfection that despite the obstacle, a calm breath, a concentrated gaze, and faith will overcome it.

Rachael is unique, a middle sister with an old soul, shy to share, yet filled with wisdom beyond her years. She is unabashedly kind, a love of all that pours from her twinkling eyes. It is this bountiful joy that brings her joy of animals to the forefront, constantly yearning for the endless love of anything on God's green earth. She is a spark of life and a deeply kind being who challenges herself to perfection, in every activity.

When I was younger, I would play sports and take dance classes like most other kids my age, yet after years of attempting at various sports and dances, I instead focused on mastering the art of music. Despite learning both the piano and cello, I eventually learned to focus my energy on what moved me: dance. See, when something moves you, bursting to get out, follow that feeling. I followed it all the way to cheer, and this is where I found a home for all my passion. It was 7th grade, and I committed to cheering on my friends, perfecting my skills, and harnessing my focus. Of course, I planned every step: I decided to take a year off of cheer so I could achieve the tumbling skills I would need for high school, and eventually make the Varsity team. Because of my decision, many of my friends and family encouraged me to follow a career path that relates to sports, but again, I found that it isn't my passion.

I thought, and thought, and thought a bit longer, and suddenly, holding my dogs in my lap, I realized what I loved more than my desires – I loved the helpless animals of the world. Of course, I would I become a veterinarian! Maybe it's because I love to help the helpless, or maybe it's because I want nothing more than to love unconditionally, but whatever the case, I am excited to carry on my education on this path.

There are many things from my childhood that I still incorporate into my life now. The life lessons of treating others as you wish to be treated and putting others before yourself are examples of how my faith has taught me to grow. The most influential figure I've had throughout my life was Grandma Lulu, because if I had an idea or thought of something I wanted to do, she wouldn't tear me down to try to convince me not to do try. Instead, she would give me advice and encourage me to pursue everything with an open heart. She also had a tremendous influence on me - I want to be as kind, elegant, and beautiful as she was. Even though she may not be with us today she still and always will have a great influence on me.

Our Rachael

Grandmothers are Forever

On a warm day in Fall,
Our Lord put out a call,
'We need a sweet girl
Not too big, not too tall.'

He sent us our Rachael,
So perfect, so new.
God knew that we'd love her
For He loved her too.

Now she's a big girl,
Growing closer to God.
He smiles on her daily
With a wink and a nod.

Grandma Lulu and Papa
<u>Our Rachael</u>

Rachael's 11th Birthday

Grandmothers are Forever

We remember tiny footprints
As you pulled yourself up from a crawl.
We remember your little girl giggles
As you learned how to walk and not fall.

Those years are now far behind you,
But to us they are like yesterday.
Each year you grow out of childhood
And leave behind your childhood ways.

We watch you change every year.
With tears we smile as you grow.
1st an infant, then a toddler, then a young girl.
You are always the sweet Rachael we know.

Papa Randy and Grandma Lulu
<u>Rachael's 11th Birthday</u>

My Darling Rachael,

I was so excited to go out with you all for your birthday dinner. Unfortunately, I am still not feeling well and the doctor wants me to wait until I see him on Tuesday before making plans. I love you so very much and am blessed beyond words to have you in my life.

Please know that I would have done anything to see you tonight. I hope to see you soon sweet Rae Rae and spend time, just the two of us.

Hugs and Kisses,
Grandma Lulu
2009

The Fun Has Just Begun

The next day Rachael helped Papa
As he started to prepare
For a small New Years Eve Party
He'll be hosting with flare.
Rachael helped answer the phone,
Papa mailed out the invites
To make sure no one is left home alone.

It's time for some fun
So Rachael runs to her horse.
She loves all animals very much,
But her favorite's the horse.

As Christmas approaches,
The fruit's fast turning ripe.
Papa picked some with Rachael,
Sweet, wet lips they did wipe.
The tangerines are bright orange and dripping with juice.
It's a good thing Grandma gave them napkins to use.

At the end of her stay, at the end of the day,
We took a moment with God
To thank Him and pray.
We thanked Him for Rachael and the fun that we've had,
We thanked Him because He provides for all we have.

Goodbye our sweet Rachael,
We sure had some fun.
Come to visit again soon
Because the fun has just begun!

Grandma Lulu
<u>The Fun Has Just Begun</u>

Sarah

Words From Sarah

Lynne Marie Sorbel, also known as Grandma Lulu, was the best Grandma that you could ever meet! She was caring, loving, sweet, and much more!

When I was first born, she was the one to care for me and was always my "go-to" for help with school. Soda, shopping, and ice cream were some of the treats that Grandma would give us, but they weren't as sweet as the time that we spent with her.

There is no reason to grieve because she is still here with us every step of the way. Even though she isn't here with us in person, she is still clapping for us, being there for us, and looking down from Heaven, smiling at her family.

When I was with my Grandma, I felt like a different person; I felt confident, happy, and beautiful. Grandma Lulu will always be in my heart.

Sarah in a Nutshell

Sarah bursts at the seams – full of life, full of words, full of heart. She is the youngest, but that has not stopped her growth, and perhaps a penchant for the center- stage land her on just that – a star of musical theater and her YouTube videos. Like her strawberry blonde hair, Sarah emanates light, bubbling, overflowing, jumping at the chance to share her thoughts, her opinions, and mostly, her stories.

She is giddy, witty, and a fountain of energy, spouting her knowledge to anyone whom will listen, and in Sarah's presence, listening is a pleasure.

I want to be a singer, mostly because I love musical theater, and of course, because I'm pretty good at it! I also want to be an English teacher like my mom. My personal plans are to be a videographer and a photographer, and I'm making these choices because it's my personality and I love these things.

I just love working on my Youtube videos, mostly because by teaching things to others, we can get better at them ourselves. It just makes sense! Going to church helped to realize that, because we can grow and help others, at the same time!

Sarah's Birth

Mommy and daddy had two little girls,
God gave them sweet faces, blue eyes and blonde curls.
But someone was missing from their family tree.
They only had Becca and Chelly you see.

It was Sossie, dear Sossie, our sweet Sarah James.
God willed it and planned it and finally she came.
From Heaven's great treasure – from so far above,
Came our precious Sarah, our Princess we love.

Like her sisters before her, her eyes are bright blue.
No blonde hair can be found though,
Hers is soft red in hue.

Happy birthday dear Sossie, we're so sad we're not there.
We send you our love and huge hugs cause we care.
We'll see you real soon, so take care little one.
May God bless you and keep you, your life's just begun.

Papa and Grandma Lulu
<u>Sarah's Birth</u>

Fairy Princess

A fairy princess is not a real thing.
Though she has gorgeous hair
And gossamer wings.

The Lord gave us a real princess
The day you were born.
Our sweet Sarah,
So precious, so beautifully formed.

You changed our whole lives
With your very first breath.
Our hearts grew three sizes – almost out of our chests.
We held you and loved you.
Each day that love grows.
Happy birthday sweet Sarah,
Our Princess, our rose.

Papa Randy and Grandma Lulu
<u>Fairy Princess</u>

Sossie Turns Four

Blue eyes so bright,
They light up the sky.
Sweet smiles so tender,
They make our eyes cry.

This is our Sossie,
Our Sarah, our Love.
Happy birthday dear Sossie,
Our gift from above.

She's now four years old,
So tall and so strong.
She knows the difference,
Between right and wrong.

She knows that we love her,
As much as we can.
I pray God will bless her,
As He blesses all man.

Grandma Lulu
<u>Sossie Turns Four</u>

Poems to the Ones Lynne Loved

Words for James

You're such a true son-in-law,
Grown strong now and wise,
Just writing this down
Brings tears to my eyes.

You're a father, a lover, a husband
For sure,
A fantastic student
Spiritual leader and more.

Our love for you grows
As the years they fly by.
You bless us all, James,
Just by being a great guy!

Lynne Sorbel
<u>Words for James</u>

Words to Shayna

On a bright summer morn,
Back in '74,
God looked down on his creation
And said, "I need something more."

"I need a sweet angel, with hair of spun gold,
She'll be spunky and playful,
A pleasure to behold."

"She must be as sweet as a peach on a vine,
She'll be kind, beautiful, and caring,
But most of all, Mine!
It took a few years before she heard my voice,
But I knew the end of the story,
And I knew she had no choice."

Now she's a mother, blessed with three precious girls,
A husband who loves her and gives her the world.
Her mom and dad think she's pretty special too,
She was their first born, their baby brand new.

For all of us who love her, too many to count,
May we wish her a birthday so special
There's no doubt.

Happy birthday sweet Shayna!

Lynne Sorbel
<u>Words to Shayna</u>

Scott's Children – Mia and Skylar Sorbel

Children are such treasured gifts.
Nothing can compare.
From the day you were born
And throughout both your lives,
This love is ours to share.

Each beautiful smile,
Every laugh, every tear.
Each day you change as you grow.
What wonderful treasures you are to us.
We pray that you always will know.

Happy First Birthday, Tendolla and Rapchokla!

Papa Randy and Grandma Lulu
<u>Scott's Children – Mia and Skylar Sorbel</u>

Grandmothers are Forever

Edward Francis Dunne – The Story of Lynne's Father

Our father, Edward Francis Dunne, was born in Dun Laoghaire, County Dublin, Ireland, on October 10th, 1926. He was the third child of six born to Patrick Dunne and Sarah Doyle. Patrick, a sailor by trade, joined the Commissioners of Irish Lights and became a midshipman stationed on the SS Isolda during World War I. On December 19, 1940, two bombs struck his ship, and he was one of six killed instantly. Our grandmother, Sarah, ever the superstitious Irish woman, swore she heard the wail of the Ban Shee at precisely the moment the ship was struck. Our father was just 14 at the time. From then on, as financial difficulties grew, our grandmother, Sarah, took in sewing from friends and neighbors in exchange for food and some small amounts of money to help the family survive. Our father would tell us of tales of when he was so hungry he would climb into other people's trash cans to retrieve partially eaten or rotten fruit and of how he would wear his one of two pairs of socks "until they stood on their own." Of course, he also "walked ten miles in the snow to school." These stories were probably only slightly exaggerated.

Blessed with great intellect and ever the motivated student, our father, vowed he would make a better life for himself. He worked hard day and night to qualify for the one full scholarship offered to a deserving student upon graduation from secondary (high) school. When his dream of achieving this scholarship was indeed realized, he immediately enrolled in law school where his Protestant girlfriend attended. Soon after, realizing he was not cut out for the law and that his very Catholic family would never accept his union with a Protestant, Edward switched to medical school instead where he eventually graduated with full honors. After graduation, he applied to numerous residencies stateside, where he knew he could make a better living.

Accepted for a position at the prestigious Cleveland Clinic in Ohio, Edward went off to America in search of his dream. After finishing an internship there, he was offered a residency at Hollywood Presbyterian Hospital where he quickly was taken under the wing of another Irish-born doctor, Redmond Chambers, who became both his mentor and close friend. It was there he eventually met his bride, Jeanne Catherine Willis. Jeanne, our mother, born on April 26, 1928, was the daughter of a close family friend of Redmond's wife, Wib (Elizabeth.) Wib's family and our mother's family had all come from Easton, Pennsylvania. Our maternal grandfather, William Alexander Willis, had come from Belfast, Ireland, much as our father had to start a new life. William died in a car accident when our mother was just ten or so, leaving the family with no income. When our mother was 13, her only sibling, Billy, an air force pilot, ten years her senior was shot down and killed, his body never recovered. Our mother lived in a house then with her mother, Estelle Apolonia Gies; her grandmother, Catherine; her Uncle Reuben; and Aunt Ada, who never married to work and helped support all the family members. Growing up during the Great Depression was a very financially difficult time for our mother and her family.

When our parents first met, our father was so poor; he could hardly afford to take our mother on a proper date. He lived in the room over Redmond and Wib's garage. But somehow the fates provided and after a seven- year- long courtship, our mother, and father, finally married. Being the good Irish Catholics they were, their eight children soon followed.

A Poem to her Father

Grandmothers are Forever

You've held my hand
You've soothed my brow.
And how you did it,
I don't know how.

You worked all day,
Drove home at dusk.
With eight eager children
Upon your lap a must!

Your patience was long
Our love never ran out
I guess that's what a real Dad
Is all about.

I'm all grown up,
I still miss my dad,
Some things never change,
And of that I'm sure glad!

Lynne Sorbel
<u>A Poem to her Father</u>

www.ingramcontent.com/pod-product-compliance
Lightning Source LLC
Chambersburg PA
CBHW041118300426
44112CB00002B/16